DONNA DAVIS LEWIS

MUSING and MEANDERING

Random Thoughts During the Pandemic

Print ISBN: 978-1-09832-386-8

eBook ISBN: 978-1-09832-387-5

Thank you to Dr. Steffanie Campbell who encouraged me to write and to Marilyn Logan, my biggest cheerleader.

POEMS

HAPPY FOR YOU

So happy for you
I really am
Your amazing love
Your pretty face
So happy for you
I really am
The perfect soufflé
The masterpiece child
Your storied career
Your FaceBook life is
All you planned
So happy for you
I really am

SOLDIER SISTER SOLEDAD

Imagine an angel with a halo of scrap
and wings sustained by truth
She fights the good fight every day even when the road is rough
Because for her... dignity, compassion and faith are enough
A child of immigrants, a mother, a wife
Brilliant, beautiful, successful
She could bask in this life
But she speaks for others who do not have her choices
And power should listen to this most eloquent of voices

35

The twins are grown now
Smart, kind, fiercely intelligent, calm, frantic, lazy, driven, loved
Perfectly imperfect sons

....

WHITE LIES

At 26 I told the truth
That haircut does not suit you
At 36 I told the truth
I disagree with your point of view
At 46 I told the truth
You will never make it there
At 56 I told the truth
I thought we should clear the air
At 66 I tell white lies
Because now I can see the world through your eyes

....

WHAT IF

What if Kaepernick brought guns to the game?
Would the Confederate flag absolve him of shame?
What if Obama played golf and ignored all who warned him?
Could he just go on TV and find someone else to blame?

....

SKIN

They wear their hate like a second skin
And I wonder, can there be any joy at all within?
To see only bad in anyone who is not like you
Must poison the heart through and through

....

SO MANY WARS

He is a veteran of many wars
The Vietcong did not despise him like
his fellow Americans did
He returned to fight the battle
to be twice as good
While privilege for so many others
was understood
But the war for justice seems
never ending
Because caring for veterans is
always pending
So he still fights today because
that is his way

HAIR

We wear it long, short, blonde, red, streaked, nappy,
relaxed, weaved, locked and Sista curled
We sacrifice paychecks, a good night's sleep,
the swimming pool
Bad hair days leave us so forlorn
We fear the mirror more than a pandemic
The salon wins but self love loses

GUILTY PLEASURES

Okay I admit it
I really like Taylor Swift
Now amongst my friends this has caused quite a riff
What about Beyoncé or Cardi B they inquire?
My answer is simple
Sometimes there's no rhyme or reason
   to the things that inspire
So I am no longer hiding out
I love Amazing Race and Survivor, Double Stuf Oreos,
People Magazine, and box wine with a spout
I like a good beach read and not the
   prestigious best seller
A Ken Burns documentary will occasionally bore me
But I can hunker down for hours watching IDTV
I'll take Target any day instead of going to Saks
What's happened to your taste level some might ask?
My guilty pleasures are just better
And those are the facts

GIRLFRIENDS

I don't have blood sisters but I do have my girls
    and you know who you are
You know when to stop me when I take the crazy too far
You're the ones who lift me up when all I can do is sink
You give me prompts to the answers when I cannot think
You always hail a masterpiece even when I color
    outside the lines
And an evening with you guarantees good times
When I write my life story, there will be a chapter for you
Telling the world you are kind and funny and
    beautiful too

FAIR WEATHER FRIEND

You were always a fair weather friend
When my life was good and yours was too
We laughed, we talked
I could always count on you
When my days were sunny and I had money and mirth to spare
You were right there
But you barely noticed when my mother died
My other friends gathered and offered comfort while I cried
When trouble found me at work but you were flying high
That cold shoulder I felt could not be denied
Then when my star rose and you needed advice
It was me that you chose
You really needed me then
That was your spin
But then you've always been a fair weather friend

DOMESTICITY

I was not blessed with the housekeeping gene
And all this joy of cooking is beyond my comprehension
But since we've all been locked down,
Cooking and cleaning are the new competitions
The thing about dusting and mopping they say
Is that you should be doing these things every day
My friends are all cleaning their closets Kondo style
Or using toothbrushes to scrub their floorboards
While I just watch TV and continue to hoard
I do not like cooking but one must do this to eat
I don't dream of new cars or fancy jewelry
A personal chef is my idea of a treat
There are those who love cooking
And a clean house makes them feel free
But for me, I get no pleasure from domesticity

FOR BOB MARLEY

Don't worry about a thing
Cause every little thing gonna be alright
Today all seems hopeless
As we struggle through each night
We pray that when we wake up
The nightmare will have ended
And there will be peace and good health as our
    Maker intended
Each day we see suffering that is impossible to tally
And we wonder when God will grant us the
    strength to rally
We are all forever changed by this terrible plight
We will need to hold on to each other
To make it through this dark night
One love, one heart
Let's get together and feel all right

THE NEW NEIGHBORHOOD

I like to go walking in the new neighborhood
Fully armed with my iPhone
Alone and wearing my jogging shoes
The houses under construction draw my attention
I compare the cabinets to the ones in my house
And marvel at the beautiful granite they use
I like to see the flooring, the window seats
    and the molding
Harmless viewing unfolding
Ahmaud did this too and was shot down at that time
Curiosity and blackness were his only crimes

FRIENDS WITH PRIVILEGE

The kids are in cages
And you said
Too bad but their parents are breaking the law
People are losing their jobs
And you said
They should have enough savings from
    which they can draw
The food lines are over reported you say
How do they run out of food in a matter of days?
They should have other resources you said
Because in this country, there is no good excuse
    for not getting ahead
And I said
It just seems to me that you have no empathy
Because not once in your life have you had to face strife

A ROSE BY ANY OTHER NAME

She named her baby girl Harper
A very popular name today
Such a White Girl name some of her friends
    were inclined to say
Little Harper could grow up to be President of the
    United States or
head of a Fortune 500 company
Sadly, the path may be easier for her than baby
    Sheniqua or Imani
Who may not get the same opportunity
Despite more impressive resumes than Olivia or Emily

LEARNING TO SWIM

My father was in the Navy during World War II
He served as a Mess Attendant
A job not befitting the smartest man I ever knew
The Greatest Generation of which he was a member
Did not see the value of this black man
As he set sail to Guam that September
He labored with other black sailors
At the U.S. Naval Supply Depot
Their story is of course largely untold
But they sacrificed much and
Helped to defeat the Japanese foe
My father never dwelled on WWII
He came home, worked hard
And fought for his due
Imagine a Navy veteran who never learned to swim
But he vowed that all his children would acquire this skill
So we all became good swimmers because that
    was his will
No, he could never teach us how to swim
Perseverance, honesty and generosity
Those were the lessons we learned from him

....

BOOMERS VS. MILLENNIALS

There is a war being waged and I am in so deep
The Boomers and the Millennials are battling
And the road to victory is steep
"Okay Boomers" they say as we wrestle with technology
And we wonder if they have any clue about the
    merits of CDs
When will you all retire so we can get promotions the
    Millennials want to know?
We Boomers say work longer hours, take less time off,
Follow the rules and your opportunities will grow
But then I looked a little closer and what did I see?
I love their sense of adventure and curiosity
I wish I'd had more of those when I was 23
They tend to accept others no matter what they look like,
Who they love or how they pray
They choose work that inspires them and maybe
    for lower pay
Because material things mean less to them at the
    end of the day
So maybe, just maybe we have no reason to fret
We can pass the ball to save our world to those
    spoiled Millennials
But wait a minute, not so fast, we are not ready yet
....

ENVY

Reading the poems of Nikki and Jericho
Leave me green with envy
Amazing wordsmiths bringing joy to many
Why can't I do that?
My friends have been married 45 years
Their love and devotion still true
Shouldn't I have a soulmate too?
My cousins have a house in the city
And another on the lake
For goodness sake
What am I doing wrong?
I am in good health
I can pay my bills
Love for family and friends is strong
But no life is perfect and I do have one flaw
For which I must atone
That is looking at my life and counting other
      people's blessings
Instead of counting my own

THE 43%

I've come to believe they really do want us all dead
They spread lies and conspiracy theories
Because in the end the vitriol puts targets on our heads
And sadly losing a few of their own tribe is no
    real sacrifice
Just collateral damage
Making America great again at any price

LETTERS FROM HOME

I miss handwritten letters signed sincerely or with love
Where the writer took the time to find just the right
    paper and pen
Those missives were sealed with a little bit of their
    heart within
When I was a girl I went away each summer to
    Girl Scout camp
My mother mailed letters perfectly timed so
    I could open one each day
A mother's love in an envelope is balm for the soul
And a life long sweet memory for the cost of a stamp

PRAYER

Is prayer enough when you're so sad you
    cannot function?
Can we pray away oppression, bigotry, marginalization
    and depression?
Prayer has brought us thus far they say
Just keep praying and one day all the pain will go away
But we cannot wait until we see heaven to claim
    what is ours
Because we have prayed we already have power
We can vote, we can march, we can believe in science,
We can scream our demands
Prayer without action leaves our destiny in others hands

....

POST OFFICE CA. 2021

It's Tuesday. No mail today.
You will have to wait until Friday.
It could be worse.
Aunt Fannie back home
must now drive on the highway
To retrieve her prescriptions and that check you sent
They're in a post office box in the next county
No more home delivery for country folks
Another connection to the world revoked
The US Post Office has been privatized
And the already rich are enjoying
their new commercial bounty
It now costs $2 to mail a letter and
The small business owner cannot afford the fees
100,000 veterans have lost their jobs
And there are those who could not care less
But the rest of us will mourn the days
When the whole civilized world agreed
The United States Postal Service
was hands down the best

....

NAVAJO LAMENT

The Navajo were here first
The colonizers brought hate and greed
And wrapped them in a bow tied package
   disguised as peace
They raped and they pillaged
And their foreign diseases sickened and decimated
But the Navajo survived even a long walk in winter
Until now history repeats
As another infectious scourge has arrived
on the wings of birds made of steel

TATTOO

I find myself longing for a tattoo
My children might be shocked
My friends would question my sanity too
A butterfly, an African proverb or maybe a teddy bear
Gracing my ankle or arm
Nothing too obviously crazy that would make
  people stare
Since it is the fashion, I don't see the harm
But as I am on the senior citizen spectrum
My midlife crisis is way past due
And needles don't thrill me
So for the moment this idea I will gladly eschew

PROCRASTINATION

Procrastination is really hope pretending to be a flaw
We put things off until tomorrow
So sure we will awaken once again
Naturally assuming that will be God's plan
He will allow us the time to wash the car, clean the oven,
do our taxes and finally call Grandma
If we were really fatalistic, we'd do everything today
Instead, next week will be just fine
Wouldn't you say?

GENEALOGY SECRETS

I would like to know if I am descended from the Yoruba,
    the Xhosa or the Zulu
What tales of home did my ancestors bring across that
    Middle Passage?
I wonder if I am an heiress to a great
    West African dynasty
Are crowns and thrones of kings and queens part of
    my legacy?
It's popular today to test your DNA to flesh out your
    origin story
With a swab of the cheek, we can now determine
If the very first rapists were English, French or German
Is there a criminal at the family reunion hiding in
    plain sight?
Do I have an extra brother somewhere?
I don't believe every secret should see the light
Some we should never share

LATE BLOOMERS

I want to talk to the late bloomers
The ones who thought their ships had sailed
And they never made it to the Gold Coast
The ones who felt unteachable, unlovable,
unable to ever reach some arbitrary goal
To them I say keep reaching, striving,
fighting for those illusive heights
This is not the time to regret
The simple truth is
You just have not peaked yet

MURDER WITNESSES

Here we go again
We're witnesses to another murder
Not enough space here to list all the names
The killers too privileged to express any shame
We know this is nothing new
400 years preceded this trend
But will it ever end?
Thank God for the cell phones that capture what's true
Though sadly they cannot guarantee the
    punishment that is due

SISTER IN SAIGON

I wanted to see Vietnam
Where so many of my brothers were lost
Fighting in remote jungles
And in the streets of Hanoi and Saigon
Where the French had once prevailed
I wondered about a country who'd lost so much
    to colonizers
Had this small country been forever stained by
    the blood of their
own people and their occupiers?
But nothing prepared me to be the novelty
A black female object of curiosity
Photographed and whispered about
But not to me unkindly

SWEET TOOTH

I've never seen a cupcake that didn't strike my fancy
Give me some flan, an eclair, ice cream or a cannoli
I know a sweet tooth is mythical but I'm here to tell you
There is no greater truth
Than my desire to indulge in sugary goodies
From jelly beans to Baby Ruths
Some travel to Italy for the gondola rides and the art
As for me, I seek the best gelato with all of my heart
New York may have Broadway but they have great
    cheesecake too
And What would New Orleans be without beignets?
Not as great as they could be I say
Alas! My doctor says eat carrot sticks because
    they are better for you
But I will still long for carrot cake with
    cream cheese frosting too!

MEN ON HORSES

A BMW, Mercedes Benz, perhaps a Tesla no less
All pretty impressive I guess
But there is something about a man on a horse
That I find sexy as hell
Somehow the man seems taller and leaner astride his
    trusted mount
And a tip of that iconic hat can cause my heart to swell
Who knows if I ever get close to a real cowboy
I might just go down for the count

SPACE FORCE

I don't really give a damn about the Space Force
Or travel to the moon or Mars
We've already screwed up this planet
No need to export our toxicity that far
Another excuse to pump billions into folly
To massage the egos of those who claim the right stuff
I am not impressed by Astronaut antics in weightlessness
I lost track a long time ago of space station missions
We've had more than enough
I prefer to see poor children with plenty to eat
And fewer homeless people lining our streets
Space travel is an expensive distraction
from the damage we've done on earth
The sick and tired do not see its worth

AMERICAN HISTORY

America is appalled at the riots in Minneapolis
Collective amnesia allows them to forget that
Violence is the American way
It is only when rioting stems from rebellion
that they profess dismay
White mobs went on the attack in Tulsa in
the Black Wall Street Massacre of 1921
Many were killed and 10,000 were left homeless that day
America looked away
The KKK is an American institution and a scourge
to all black people
They have bombed, burned, lynched and
castrated while their members pretended to pray
America looked away
So why is anyone surprised when people grow weary
and have nothing else to lose?
They resist in the way America teaches them each and
every day

HATS

Some women look incredible in hats
I am not one of them
The last hat that flattered me
Was the Easter bonnet I wore at the age of 3
What a joy it must be to step out on the town
Sporting a jaunty chapeaux
Yet as much as I love seeing my friends wear hats
My inner voice tells me no
From a cute little Raspberry beret to a Church Lady
　　straw confection
I've tried them all you see
But instead of sitting atop my head like a crown
A hat makes me look like a clown

I DO LOVE DOGS

This poem will get me into trouble with some
  of my best friends
I do love dogs but not too much and your dogs especially
Between gourmet chicken breast meals and
  $100 hair cuts
You've spoiled your dogs completely
The dogs have more toys than Princess Charlotte,
  favorite TV channels,
And beds made of memory foam
My childhood dog was Molly who strolled
  through our neighborhood
tagged but unleashed and she always found
  her way home
I miss the days when dogs were beloved but still free
And the only spoiled person in the house was me

HAPPIER

I'm happier today
Happier than I should be
The streets are aflame
Infection is raging
Cops are killing my people
But I'm happier than I should be
There is nothing I can do in my small sphere
To make things any better
Finally I have gained the proverbial wisdom to
    know that hate will go unfettered
And I cannot change the hearts of people who
    will never see my value
Happiness is so easy when you recognize the
    limits of your power
And accept that no help will come from those
    in the Ivory Tower
I'm happier than I should be and that truly
    makes me free

··

BODY IMAGE

Oh how powerful is the mirror
Capturing the true image
But never the one we treasure
Even though it might give others pleasure
The one we want is slimmer or taller
Or has bigger breasts or maybe smaller
We long for more of this or less of that
We've grown way too old to claim baby fat
No, now we are just fat Baby
And we should be okay with that
Still we continue to pine for our 25 year old self
The one with the trim hips and thighs
But when that girl looked into the mirror
She too saw only flaws
And not the beautiful imperfection
Right there in her own reflection

··

MEDITATION

I hoped meditation would make me a better person
More compassionate
More selfless
Able to let go of regrets
Each day I sat very still
And centered my mind on the now
Tried to cancel emotional debts
Recited my mantras like vows
But my mind would not cooperate
I wondered if the monkey brain
Would always be my fate
Jumping and pouncing on this idea or that
Fretting and blaming myself even as I sat on my mat
But some say practice makes perfect
If you just persevere
Well no one is perfect
Not even the Dalai Lama I fear
So I keep practicing meditation
With mindfulness as my North Star
Now, not every day is peaceful
but so many more are

BOYCOTT

I used to love Hobby Lobby
A modern day version of a five and dime store
Filled with picture frames, trinkets and notions
And sculptures made of resin
An All American store where all the goods
    are made in China
Including the United States flags
No matter the holiday or the season or the party plan
I could fill my basket with candles, silk flowers,
    bonbons and more
I really did love that store
But then I found out Hobby Lobby is the devil
So I don't go there anymore
They want to deny their employees access to healthcare
They've stolen religious artifacts
And just like all bad guys they know how to
    cover their tracks
But here is my dilemma when considering a boycott
What is a well meaning person to do?
When so many other corporations are evil too

PRONOUNS

I have a new young friend
Who I really don't want to offend
I said Who in that sentence
But should it be Whom?
This language we speak is really not that pure
I try to be correct both politically and grammatically
But it is not easy
My friend says I should always refer to her as She
This seems so obvious to me
But now I have learned I must choose the proper
      gender pronoun
Or risk offending someone's identity
Him, Her, They, Their, He, She
It seems the proper list is long
So please forgive me if I get it wrong

MISAPPROPRIATED

Our culture is being misappropriated they say
But I don't really care about that
If it would stop discrimination
I would gladly give it all away
You say you love our music
And the cornrows in our hair
You plump up your lips with collagen
And pad your butts like the Kardashians
But what about the struggles that America
    feels are our due
Will you appropriate them too?

MY LAST BOYFRIEND

He left early in the morning
I would not say he was the one that got away
He went away
Quietly
He left as he came
No fanfare
No tears
Bound together by habit
Not love
The mutual fear of growing old alone
Not enough to inspire desire

HOPE

I think the camel's back has finally been broken
And now it's okay to hope
There is a new generation of activists
Very young and very brave
Black, brown, yellow and white
They have nothing and everything to lose
And they are unafraid
And yes they do want America to be great
They are just not willing to wait

APOLOGIES

These high profile apologies amuse me
Dripping in faux sincerity
With eyes on their bottom lines
Held in high esteem because they can throw a ball
Or sing a song
Role models for modern times
"I'm so sorry I said it
My words got twisted
But never my heart
May I please have a brand new start?
I promise I'm one of the good guys"
But when they first open their mouths
They are speaking their truth
I just smile
And wait for them to apologize

MR. RIGHT

I am still looking for Mr. Right
I've been on all the dating apps
Including the ones for senior citizens
I am not holding my breath for this mythical Mister
I just go on living my life like most of my sisters
Standing up again when I fall
And celebrating all of my wins
You will find him in church one woman said
Although she found her own husband in her
    best friend's bed
Others say you must be more social
Get out of the house
Well I like what I like and I go out a lot to have fun
Usually surrounded by a room full of women
    in search of a spouse
I read of a woman who married at 78
So I am not giving up
Maybe my Mr. Right is just running late

STRONG

I wish you'd told me I was beautiful
That my spirit awakened your soul
I wished you'd remembered when I stood by you
Nurtured you
Encouraged you
Helped you write your story
The one you used to be great for all the others
But no, you told me I was strong
I'd be alright on my own
Strong enough to make my way alone
Of course what you said was true
I made a very good life without you
But being strong is so exhausting

THE BLACK FRIEND

There's one in almost every romantic comedy
Brassy and fun, full of good advice
Included in the plot just to help the female lead win
That omnipresent character better known as
The Black Friend
The Black Friend is cool and rarely gets angry
She would never upset the apple cart
And no one really cares
What's actually in her heart
Like a favorite pair of earrings or the reliable
      little black dress
The Black Friend can be invited to the brunch
      or the cocktail party
Bringing minimal stress
Intelligent and witty
Always ready with some wisdom
And an acceptable point of view
I have first hand knowledge of this woman
Because I've been the Black Friend a time or two

SMARTER

I always wanted to be smarter
I really don't understand this culture of glorifying dumb
Where is this coming from?
Education is being disparaged as only for elites
Instead of reading books we get our
    information from tweets
Faced with facts
People prefer to believe a conspiracy theory
Evidence of truth is treated with disdain
Revisionist history is making me weary
Common sense and intellect are no longer
    American values
The badge of stupidity is worn proudly
Like a new pair of shoes

....

THE MAYORS

Black Girl Magic really is a thing
The Mayors are stepping up
Keisha, Lori, London and Vi
Muriel and LaToya
Big city mayors making tough decisions
Speaking truth to power
Fierce, compassionate, working hard and smart
And not forgetting that a true leader should
    also have a heart

....

....

FOR ELIJAH

I'm an introvert and I'm different he said
And he could not breathe
Slight and looking even younger than his 23 years
He was not a football player, a hip hop star,
    or an object of fear
He was a curious child
Who became a vegetarian
A massage therapist who played the violin
Introverted and sweetly different
Denied the simple right of breath
I can only imagine how his mother must have wept

....

YOU

Only you could turn the death
of someone we all loved into your story
Your pain is always deeper
Your sorrow more intense
No one else can feel like you feel
You not only flaunt your feelings
You extinguish all of ours
Your best friend is hurting
His bond with his wife is slipping
But you can't see his suffering
Because you say you never liked her anyway
How hard is it to just one time keep the You at bay
And listen with an open heart to what others have to say?

POINTS OF VIEW

You've traveled the world she said
And I have
You drink the right wine with your dinner
Sometimes I do
You know about film, opera, books and ballet
A little bit of knowledge is dangerous I say
You have a beautiful face
A long happy marriage
I remind her
A lovely home
Money in the bank lets you do what you want to
Whose life is more beautiful depends on
    your point of view

....

FOR CANDACE

How sad it must be to wake up each morning
Remembering who you are
And hating the very idea of it
To look into the mirror and not see an intelligent,
    beautiful black face
Instead you see an apology for your race
Self loathing is your occupation
You seek gratification from your oppressors
And claim money and infamy from deplorable
    people in our nation
What happened to you to siphon all the joy
    from your self identification?

....

OPTIMISTIC

Always joyful
Eternally optimistic
She never sees the pitfalls
There is no dark side in her world
I do love her dearly
But sometimes I just have to avoid that girl
Now and then I need a fellow scowler
And it helps if she's witty
Together we can agree
Life can be really shitty
We look at the universe and see the end of days
And know we're going to hell because of our ugly ways

WHITE JESUS

When Jesus returns
Will people be disappointed if his hair is not blonde
And his eyes are not blue?
He was born in the Middle East and was most
    certainly was a Jew
Probably had coarse black hair,
    brown skin and brown eyes
Unlike the images on Hallmark cards and the
    stain glass windows we prize
He will look just like the people unwelcome in the homes
of so many Christians today
Will they refuse to join the Rapture in dismay?

SHE ASKED US TO PRAY

She asked us all to pray
To pray away the gay
When her son came to her for love
She could not offer it unconditionally
So she asked for help from above
She could not see her gift from God
Was there before her very eyes
Instead she asked us all to pray
That he could learn to live his life with lies
She asked us all to pray
And that is what we do
Dear God please grant this fine young man
His mother's love today

BLACK CONSERVATIVES

I suppose it's possible to be a Black Conservative
Without clinging to self hatred, denial or buffoonery
Although one or more of these traits appear
    to be required
I won't be mean and call it coonery
But there is a common trait I see
It's that genuine belief they all seem to possess
that everything they have is theirs because they
    earned it on their own
They believe even the bricks and the bats
    America uses to bash us
have nothing to do with the color of our skin
All we have to do is work harder and we will win
They never see the "we" in our struggle to get ahead
They don't lift up their brothers and sisters
They blame them for their troubles instead
They owe Affirmative Action for their fancy degrees
Yet they hide out on the Supreme Court and in the Senate
And gleefully work to bring their own people to
    their knees

DO YOU

Be You!
Do You!
For You!
Easier to say today
Than at age 19 when just being you seems odd
Every family has that one member
   who does not quite fit the mold
They are loved fiercely but their choices
   seem a little too bold
My Auntie Lil joined the Great Migration in 1941
She left Texas for Chicago and left her family stunned
Such bravery and independence was like
   nothing they had seen
But when she came home with a real career
She became the family Queen

IRREDEEMABLE

Some people are irredeemable
Their souls forever lost
They go through life
Proud of taking the low road
Always angry at someone, some group, some other
Unable or unwilling to see the pain of another

FOR A BLACK GIRL

They say you're so pretty for a black girl
They say we have to fight for our black boys
Because they are endangered in this cruel world
And they are
But what of the little black girls taunted for their bodies,
their voices, their hair
What of their despair?
They say you're really smart for a black girl
I say you are beautiful and brilliant and fearless
Let your victory flag unfurl black girl!

OPPOSITES ATTRACT

We were all shocked when they got married
No one in our circle had any clue
Tongues started wagging
Never knew them to even date, did you?
She is cerebral and preternaturally calm
Long legged and lean
Her aura pristine
She earned her degrees, traveled the world,
     and took many lovers
Came back to our hometown to care for her mother
He wears an ever present fedora and a perpetual smile
A small man, short, wiry and thin
Served time in the pen
Fathered children out of his marriage and within
But a kinder person I have never met
Every life has some regrets
It is a sweet conundrum that these two people found love
But when I see them together
I can see their devotion is not an act
It can be quite beautiful when opposites attract

....

THE ODD GIRL

My mother-in-law used to say
She's a very sweet girl but a bit odd, don't you agree?
Maybe if she did something with that hair
   or that makeup
Or those clothes
A little red lipstick would flatter her immensely
Or even a little powder on her nose
She's a very smart girl but a little cheeky, don't you think?
So opinionated, so rash, nothing ever left unstated
I loved my mother-in-law with all of my heart
No one laughed harder at my jokes
Or cried more when my marriage fell apart
But looking back now, and truth be told
Maybe I was the odd girl of whom she spoke

....

AMERICA THE BEACON

America is still a beacon for some
Kwame from Ghana was my Uber driver
And that was not his only job
He was a student, a pharmacy tech, and a yard man
The antithesis of a lazy immigrant
Looking forward to the 4th of July to read his
     citizenship pledge
So sure that being an American would give him an edge
Lured by the promise of prosperity
Inspired by the fervor of Americans when they pray
Undeterred by the irony that Black Americans
are still waiting for their Independence Day

CODE SWITCHING

We are all experts at switching code
Our stints in corporate America taught us to
    easily slip into that mode
But there's a cultural lifeboat we reach for when need to
    connect to our tribes
Yes, we know how to enunciate and speak picture
    perfectly grammatically
We can turn down the volume to fit in depending
    on the situation, you see
We may laugh or talk a little less freely lest we offend
But at brunch with our girls in the newly gentrified hood
Or on Saturday nights playing spades with our cousins
We can just be ourselves and it feels so damn good

MY FIRST BEST FRIEND

My mother was my first best friend
Together me made popcorn balls and planted roses
and hemmed the skirts of homemade dresses
But like a lot of beautiful things,
    that great friendship came to an end
The teenage years were the kiss of death to that
    unshakable bond
I was convinced I was so much smarter than she
    could ever be
Nothing she could do was good enough to
    satisfy that younger me
My beloved mother became the enemy
Then something truly amazing happened and
    I can't say exactly when
Maybe it was during one of those times
when only my mother could quench my tears
Or maybe on a day when we both laughed hard
at all of our old foibles through the years
When my father died I became her plus one
And oh the shock! She was so much fun!
And when her long and full life came to its quiet end
I looked at my mother and saw my first and
    last best friend

THE 80S

50 is the new 30 or so they say
Well I'm way past 50 and feeling like 80 today
Bones creaking
Sinuses leaking
Anticipating another day in my chair
My wine glass sits conveniently there
I guess 80 is the new 60 now
And I really am feeling the pressure swell
Maxine Waters, Ruth Bader Ginsburg,
 Tina Turner and Nancy Pelosi
Are collectively raising hell
These women in their 80s are out there killin'
While I sit in front of the TV chillin'
But as soon as I've binge watched everything on Netflix
and rewatched The Green Mile
I promise to do something worthwhile

ANTI BLACKNESS

My beautiful, brilliant Nigerian friend uses
   bleaching cream
to lighten her lovely skin
I'd guess the same could be said of Beyoncé, Rihanna and
Sammy Sosa to name a few
This is hardly a novel trend
Colorism is nothing new
Across Africa, South Asia and North America
Sadly, fair skin is still the ideal
There is a multi billion dollar market for lotions,
   creams and peels
Used to eradicate the vestiges of darkness and
   bolster self esteem
Imagine possessing beauty, intelligence, talent
   and prosperity
but a lighter complexion is still your biggest dream
It seems the colonizers will continue to win
As long as we choose anti blackness
   when we look at our own skin

A LONG TIME COMING

There have been times that I thought
   I couldn't last for long
But now I think I'm able to carry on
It's been a long time coming
But I know a change is gonna come, oh yes it will*
Born in the 50s
Growing up in the 60s
A lifetime recruit in this war to be free
I can finally see something on the horizon that
   resembles liberty
I may not live to see the happy ending
   that was the vision of MLK
But things are happening in our nation
   that do leave me some hope
That the change our parents prayed for is possible today

*Lyrics from *A Change is Gonna Come* by Sam Cooke written in 1964

Donna Davis Lewis retired as a Travel Consultant during the 2020 pandemic. She is passionate about travel, food, wine and movies. An inveterate political junkie, she believes in social action and doing good wherever she can. This is her first book of poetry.